T0197669

31 DAYS OF PRAISE

Daily Prayer Affirmations

Dr. Alexis Hamlor

Scripture quotations marked NIV are taken from the Holy Bible, New International Version®. NIV®. Copyright © 1973, 1978, 1984 by International Bible Society. Used by permission of Zondervan. All rights reserved. [Biblica]

To order additional copies of this book, contact:
Xlibris
844-714-8691
www.Xlibris.com
Orders@Xlibris.com

ISBN: Softcover   978-1-6698-4521-8
       Hardcover   978-1-6698-4522-5
       EBook   978-1-6698-4518-8

Print information available on the last page

Rev. date: 02/21/2024

31 DAYS OF PRAISE

Alexis Hamlor

31 DAYS OF PRAISE

"Therefore I tell you, whatever you ask in prayer, believe that you have received it, and it will be yours."

-Mark 11:24

31 DAYS OF PRAISE

Hello Beautiful Family,

Thank you for choosing to pick up this book and read its contents. These daily prayers and affirmations are an addition to the previous volume of 31 Days of Praise-The ABCs of Faith. God gave me instruction in making this into a companion book to supplement the previous daily devotionals.

Utilize the daily prayer affirmations to spiritually awaken your heart, mind, and soul. Remember to always speak positive words of faith and hope into your current situation. I pray you are blessed with confidence and strength as you walk into newness and oneness with God.

As always, I AM praying and pressing forward right along with you.

I love you all so much...Stay Encouraged and HappyReading!

God Bless You Family!

TABLE OF CONTENTS

DAY 1
A-Anointed

I AM an anointed vessel of God,

I AM worthy of all the gifts that God has for my life,

My ANOINTING is a blessing that brings healing to others.

Let us pray,

Father, I thank you for the anointing that you have given unto me. I pray that I may continue to have favor in your eyes and use my anointing according to Your Will. In Jesus' name I pray. Amen.

Scripture Reflection:
Psalm 105:15 "Do not touch My anointed ones and do My prophets no harm." (NIV).

DAY 2
B-Beautiful

I AM a beautiful creation,

I AM bold, beautiful, and full of greatness,

My BEAUTY shines from the inside out.

Let us pray,
Lord, thank you for creating me in your image and likeness. Help me to embrace the beauty of every encounter that I have with others today. Amen.

Scripture Reflection:
Ecclesiastes 3:11 "He has made everything beautiful in its time. He has also set eternity in the human heart; yet[a] no one can fathom what God has done from beginning to end." (NIV).

DAY 3
C-Chosen

I AM the chosen one,

I AM choosing to use my gifts and calling to shed light in dark places.

I AM called by God, and I choose His will for my life.

Let us pray,
Father, thank you for choosing me to be a blessing unto others. Lord, walk with me and allow my light to shine so that others will see your marvelous light in and through me. In Jesus' name. Amen.

Scripture Reflection:
1 Peter 2:9 "But you are a chosen people, a royal priesthood, a holy nation, God's special possession, that you may declare the praises of him who called you out of darkness into his wonderful light." (NIV).

DAY 4
C-Caring

I AM a caring and considerate person,

I AM careful and courteous in what I say and do towards others .

I will not allow anxiety or fear to hold me back, for I know that God truly cares for me.

Let us pray,
Father, thank you for being my strong tower in the time of need. Help me to always remember that I can seek your face despite what I am going through. Thank you for caring about my every need. Amen.

Scripture Reflection:
1 Peter 5:7 "Cast all your anxiety on him because he cares for you." (NIV).

DAY 5
D-Destined

I AM destined for goodness and greatness,

I AM determined to live each day of my life to the fullest.

My destiny cannot be limited or shaken by anyone, for I know that God orders my step each day.

Let us pray,
Lord, thank you for preparing the way for me. I can walk in the power and authority you have given me, as I walk into my destiny. Amen.

Scripture Reflection:
1 Corinthians 2:7 "No, we declare God's wisdom, a mystery that has been hidden and that God destined for our glory before time began." (NIV).

DAY 6
E-Elevating

I AM evolving and elevating in order to reach my destiny,

I AM climbing higher heights spiritually and naturally

My elevation is credited to God, who exalts me according to His will.

Let us pray,
Father, you said if we be humbled, then you would exalt us in due time. Thank you for elevating me in this season, and I ask that you continue to use me for your glory and honor, in Jesus' name. Amen.

Scripture Reflection:
Esther 3:1 "After these events, King Xerxes honored Haman son of Hammedatha, the Agagite, elevating him and giving him a seat of honor higher than that of all the other nobles." (NIV).

DAY 7
F-Fearless

I AM fearless and covered by the blood of the lamb,

I AM not fearful or afraid of any trap the enemy tries to set before me.

My God is able to deliver me from any snares or tricks that my haters try to plot against me.

Let us pray,
Father, I want to say thank you for giving me the spirit of boldness. I will not walk in fear because you have given me the strength to face any circumstance. I bless You both now and forevermore. Amen.

Scripture Reflection:
Hebrews 13:6 "So that we fearlessly say, "The Lord is my helper; I will not be afraid: what can man do to me?" (NIV).

DAY 8
F-Faithful

I AM a faithful prayer warrior,

I AM faithful unto God and demonstrate his love and compassion towards others.

My faithfulness is pleasing to God, and He openly rewards me for my obedience and service.

Let us pray,
Lord, thank you for helping me to remain steadfast and unmovable in my daily walk. Please help me to walk faithfully and be an example unto others. Amen.

Scripture Reflection:
Deuteronomy 32:4 "He is the Rock, his works are perfect, and all his ways are just. A faithful God who does no wrong, upright and just is he." (NIV).

DAY 9
G-Grateful

I AM grateful for each day that I am blessed to see,

I AM grateful for the people, places, and things that I have and will experience.

My gratefulness keeps me humble and loving towards others.

Let us pray,
Dear Lord, I just want to say thank you with a grateful and thankful heart. You are so awesome and amazing, and I appreciate everything that you have done for me. Amen.

Scripture Reflection:
Psalm 147:7 "Sing to the Lord with grateful praise; make music to our God on the harp." (NIV).

DAY 10
H-Hopeful

I AM hopeful about my present and future goals,

I AM hopeful that tomorrow will bring new blessings.

My hopefulness gives me the confidence to face any of the challenges that seem impossible.

Let us pray,
Father, thank you for giving me hope and determination to push through any and every situation. I bless you for your love and guidance. Amen.

Scripture Reflection:
Romans 12:12 "Be joyful in hope, patient in affliction, faithful in prayer." (NIV).

DAY 11
I- Immaculate

I AM immaculate and perfectly imperfect.

I AM forgiven by God, and He has washed away my sins and made me brand new.

My immaculate image frees me from past mistakes, and allows me to move forward by faith.

Let us pray,
Father, thank you for washing me clean, and making me whole. I can now step into the new life and fulfill the promises that you have for my life. Amen.

Scripture Reflection:
Peter 3:14 "So then, dear friends, since you are looking forward to this, make every effort to be found spotless, blameless and at peace with him." (NIV).

DAY 12

J- Just Right

I AM a beautiful person that was made just right,

I AM God's creation and He made me in His image and likeness.

My God has blessed me with the talents and abilities to do everything that I put my mind to. Everything about me was made just right.

Let us pray,
Father, I am so thankful for you making me as one of your amazing creations. You have made me just right and I am so happy to be called your own. Amen.

Scripture Reflection:
Psalm 11:7 "For the Lord is righteous, he loves justice; the upright will see his face." (NIV).

DAY 13
K- Kind

I AM a kind and compassionate person,

I AM kind and caring towards my brothers and sisters everyday.

My kindness allows me to see the good in others, despite how others may perceive their demeanor.

Let us pray,
Lord, I thank you for always showing me love and kindness every day. Your kindness gives me the courage to embrace and love those around me. Thank you so much for your presence in my life. Amen.

Scripture Reflection:
Ephesians 4:32 "Be kind and compassionate to one another, forgiving each other, just as in Christ God forgave you." (NIV).

DAY 14
L- Loving

I AM a loyal and loving person that allows my light to shine brightly.

I AM loving and share my love with those who are deserving of it.

My loving ways are demonstrated in how I act, react, and treat my fellowman.

Let us pray,
Father, I know what love is because of You. You have shown me the greatest love of all and because of that I am able to love those around me, and even turn the other cheek when necessary. Thank you Lord. Amen.

Scripture Reflection:
Psalm 144:2 "He is my loving God and my fortress, my stronghold and my deliverer, my shield, in whom I take refuge, who subdues peoples under me." (NIV).

DAY 15
M- Motivated

I AM motivated to achieve my dreams, goals, and aspirations.

I AM motivated to take a leap of faith and move ahead in the right direction.

My motivation allows me to stay focused and keep moving forward with a clear vision.

Let us pray,
Father, you said that I should write the vision for my life and make it plain. Thank you for keeping me motivated and focused on the blessings that you have in store for me. Amen.

Scripture Reflection:
Hebrews 10:24 "And let us consider how we may spur one another on toward love and good deeds." (NIV).

DAY 16
N- Never Alone

I AM never alone because Jesus walks with me everyday.

I AM never by myself, no matter how many times I have to walk alone physically.

My Father in heaven leads and guides my footsteps and He reminds me of His presence on a daily basis.

Let us pray,
Father, every time I feel lonely I thank you for reminding me of the footprints in the sand. Lord, continue to carry me through every situation that I am faced with in this life. Amen.

Scripture Reflection:
Hebrews 13:5 "Keep your lives free from the love of money and be content with what you have, because God has said, "Neverwill I leave you; never will I forsake you." (NIV).

DAY 17
O-Overjoyed

I AM overjoyed and satisfied with the fullness of life.

I AM overjoyed and happy about the fulfillment of the promises that God has destined for me.

My ability to enjoy the simple pleasures of life keeps me grounded and content.

Let us pray,
Heavenly Father, thank you for giving me an unspeakable joy. I am overjoyed with the new mercies that You have given me everyday. Amen.

Scripture Reflection:
1 Peter 4:13 "But rejoice inasmuch as you participate in the sufferings of Christ, so that you may be overjoyed when his glory is revealed." (NIV).

DAY 18
P-Positive

I AM a positive, prosperous, vessel of God.

I AM a positive, pure being, that exhibits a noble and upright attitude.

My positive vibes attract other souls to me.

Let us pray,
Father, thank you for keeping me in perfect peace. Allow me to stay positive and see the good in everything around me. Amen.

Scripture Reflection:
Philippians 4:8 "Finally, brothers and sisters, whatever is true, whatever is noble, whatever is right, whatever is pure, whatever is lovely, whatever is admirable—if anything is excellent or praiseworthy—think about such things." (NIV).

DAY 19
P-Patient

I AM a patient, calm, and understanding person.

I AM patient and considerate of the feelings and opinions of others.

My patience allows me to remain true to myself and never act out of character in times of trouble.

Let us pray,
Father, thank you keeping me patient. Lord, I appreciate your patience with me. Help me to stay patient in waiting on Your perfect timing. Amen.

Scripture Reflection:
Romans 12:12 "Be joyful in hope, patient in affliction, faithful in prayer." (NIV).

DAY 20

Q- Quick to Forgive

I AM quick to forgive others who have sinned against me.

I AM able to forgive in love, and not hold grudges against anyone.

My ability to forgive keeps me in a place of love, peace, and contentment.

Let us pray,
Father, I am able to forgive and let go of past hurts, because I want to move ahead in life. Thank you for giving me the mindset to forgive and forget, in Jesus' name I pray. Amen.

Scripture Reflection:
Colossians 3:13 "Bear with each other and forgive one another if any of you has a grievance against someone. Forgive as the Lord forgave you." (NIV).

DAY 21
R-Redeemed

I AM redeemed by the blood of Jesus.

I AM redeemed and set free from all past hurts, mistakes, and bad decisions.

My God has redeemed me and I know that He is leading me in a divinely aligned manner.

Let us pray,
Father, I know that You are my true redeemer. You live and have given me the strength to live a life that is guilt-free. Thank you so much Lord. Amen.

Scripture Reflection:
Psalm 107:2 "Let the redeemed of the Lord tell their story– those he redeemed from the hand of the foe."
(NIV).

DAY 22
S-Successful

I AM a successful and blessed servant of the Most High God.

I AM successful in my everyday endeavors.

My success is not determined by man, for God is the only one who controls my fate.

Let us pray,
Father, thank you for the success that You have allowed me to achieve. I pray that You continue to lead me towards future successes, in Jesus' name I thank you and praise you. Amen.

Scripture Reflection:
Joshua 1:7 "Be strong and very courageous. Be careful to obey all the law my servant Moses gave you; do not turn from it to the right or to the left, that you may be successful wherever you go." (NIV).

DAY 23
S-Strong

I AM much stronger today, than I was yesterday.

I AM a strong and courageous individual.

My daily prayers give me the strength to face another day.

Let us pray,
Father, thank you for making me strong, willing, and able to take on any challenges that may come about in this life. Help me to exercise my faith and build up that muscle in making it stronger each day. Amen.

Scripture Reflection:
1 Corinthians 1:25 "For the foolishness of God is wiser than human wisdom, and the weakness of God is stronger than human strength." (NIV).

DAY 24
T-Trustworthy

I AM a trustworthy, truthful person that doesn't spread lies.

I AM trustworthy and stay true to others with honest words that bring about empowerment.

My trustworthiness is an honorable characteristic that allows others to feel safe in opening up to me.

Let us pray,
Father, thank you for helping me to stay true and honest towards those around me. Keep me humbled, while also remembering to trust and obey You. Amen.

Scripture Reflection:
Psalm 19:7 "The law of the Lord is perfect, refreshing the soul. The statutes of the Lord are trustworthy, making wise the simple." (NIV).

DAY 25
U-Understanding

I AM an understanding, unbreakable force to be reckoned with.

I AM understanding and sensitive towards the needs of others.

My understanding and sensitivity makes me relatable in discerning delicate situations with clarity.

Let us pray,
Dear Lord, thank you for giving me understanding to empathize with those around me. Allow me to continue shedding love and light to all, in Jesus' name I pray. Amen.

Scripture Reflection:
Philippians 4:7 "And the peace of God, which transcends all understanding, will guard your hearts and your minds in Christ Jesus." (NIV).

DAY 26

V-Victorious

I AM victorious and triumphant in conquering all of my fears.

I AM victorious in battle; I allow God to fight for me.

My victories all belong to God, He allows my enemies to be my footstool.

Let us pray,
Father, thank you for fighting every situation on my behalf. You keep me in perfect peace in the midst of all turbulence, and make my biggest enemies behave. Thank you for your love and support. Amen.

Scripture Reflection:
Psalm 20:6 "Now this I know: The Lord gives victory to his anointed. He answers him from his heavenly sanctuary with the victorious power of his right hand." (NIV).

DAY 27
W-Wise

I AM a wise, intelligent, and intuitive person.

I AM wise and prayerful in making important decisions concerning my life.

My wisdom and knowledge has shaped my spiritual growth in this journey.

Let us pray,
Father, thank you for giving me spiritual wisdom everyday. This wisdom keeps me wise and undefeated, no matter what I face in life. Amen.

Scripture Reflection:
Proverbs 29:11 "Fools give full vent to their rage, but the wise bring calm in the end." (NIV).

DAY 28

W-Willing

I AM willing to take chances and make mistakes with humility and faith.

I AM willing to listen to others so that I can learn new things that will help me to grow.

My willingness to accept others keeps me open to new blessings and alternate perspectives.

Let us pray,
Father, thank you for gifting me with the spirit of willingness. Teach me to stay humble and willing to love, cherish, and uplift those around me, in Jesus' name I pray. Amen.

Scripture Reflection:
Isaiah 1:19 "If you are willing and obedient, you will eat the good things of the land." (NIV).

DAY 29

X-Xperienced

I AM an experienced and seasoned son/daughter of God.

I AM experienced and proud of the lessons that I've learned over time.

My experiences and life lessons have shaped my character and abilities to move forward with positivity.

Let us pray,
Father, thank you for the experiences that You have allowed me to go through. I am learning how to be stronger throughout this process, while remaining stable and grounded in You. Amen.

Scripture Reflection:
Joshua 24:31 "Israel served the Lord throughout the lifetime of Joshua and of the elders who outlived him and who had experienced everything the Lord had done for Israel." (NIV).

DAY 30
Y- Yield

I AM learning how to yield not to temptation.

I AM yielding unto the will of God in my life.

My yielding is not in vain; I am learning how to strive and seek the truth in everything.

Let us pray,
Father, thank you for allowing me to yield to Your will and to Your way. Help me to fight off the everyday temptations that try to distract me. Keep me focused and determined to do the right thing. Amen.

Scripture Reflection:
Proverbs 8:19 "My fruit is better than fine gold; what I yield surpasses choice silver." (NIV).

DAY 31
Z-Zealous

I AM zealous, eager, and passionate about life.

I AM zealous about the blessings that are springing forth, with my name on it.

My zeal comes from knowing that God is in complete control of my life and He directs my path.

Let us pray,
Father, thank you for giving me zeal and excitement about my present and future circumstances. I can face another day knowing that You are steadily watching over me. Amen.

Scripture Reflection:
Proverbs 23:17 "Do not let your heart envy sinners, but always be zealous for the fear of the Lord." (NIV).

Special Thanks

Thank you to everyone who has decided to read and affirm these daily prayer affirmations over their lives. My prayer is that God will give you the strength, confidence, and sound mind to press forward with the plans that He has for your lives. Be encouraged family, love you all dearly. Until next time...

God Bless Family!

Love Always,
Alexis Hamlor

Alexis Hamlor is an African-American authoress from the Bronx, N.Y. Alexis enjoys teaching, traveling, cooking, and writing. She has recently completed a Doctoral degree in Education and continues to spread her love of God through devotional inspiration.

For other releases, check out the digital formats available on Amazon, Amazon Kindle, Google Play, Apple I-tunes, Barnes & Noble, and Xlibris website.

31 Days of Praise: Two Minute Devotionals Vol. 1

31 Days of Praise: A Closer Walk Vol. II

31 Days of Praise: Draw Me Closer Vol.III

31 Days of Praise: The ABCs of Faith Vol. IV

Printed in the United States
by Baker & Taylor Publisher Services